THE MEGA BOOK OF KIDS' JOKES

ARCTURUS

This edition published in 2009 by Arcturus Publishing Limited
26/27 Bickels Yard, 151–153 Bermondsey Street,
London SE1 3HA

ISBN: 978-1-84837-358-7
CH000676US

Printed in Singapore

Design and Illustration by CREATIVE QUOTIENT

Compiler: Anna Amari-Parker
Editor: Rebecca Gerlings

CONTENTS

Dear reader, a word of advice: Hold onto your head—this book'll make you laugh it right off!

Packed with hundreds of rib-tickling, side-splitting, eye-watering, cheek-aching gags, it guarantees hours of amusement that will have you and your friends rolling around with laughter. Whether nutty names or knock, knocks are your thing, or you like nothing better than a painfully funny pun, with so many jokes to choose from there's something here for everyone!

NUTTY NAMES

What do you call a doctor who operates without anesthetic on her nieces and nephews ?

An agony aunt !

What do you call a man whose dad was a canon ?

A son of a gun !

What do you call a man with two left feet ?

Whatever you like—if he tries to catch you he'll just run round in circles !

What do you call a bee who is always complaining ?

A grumble bee !

What do you call a Roman emperor with a cold ?

Julius Sneezer !

What do you call a man with a cable coming out of his ear ?

Mike !

What do you call a man who does everything at top speed ?

Max !

What do you call a magician's assistant ?

Trixie !

What do you call a man who goes fishing every weekend ?

Rod !

What do you call a teacher who wears earplugs ?

Anything you like—he can't hear you !

What do you call a failed lion tamer ?

Claude Bottom !

What do you call a man and woman who show you up in front of your friends ?

Mom and Dad !

NUTTY NAMES

What do you call twin brothers with drums on their heads ?

Tom, Tom !

What do you call a man who likes drawing and painting ?

Art !

What do you call a 490-pound wrestler ?

Whatever he tells you to !

Who is the patron saint of toys ?

Saint Francis of a seesaw !

What's the name of that really strict teacher ?

Miss Norder—Laura Norder !

What do you call a man who works in a perfume shop at Christmas ?

Frank in Scents !

What do you call a woman who only comes out at Christmas ?

Carol !

What do you call a woman who checks punctuation ?

Dot !

What do you call a man with seagulls on his head ?

Cliff !

What do you call a man who keeps rabbits ?

Warren !

What do you call a man who has pet rabbits and writes huge novels ?

Warren Peace !

NUTTY NAMES

An automobile salesman called his first daughter Toyah, then he called his second daughter Toyah as well…

She was the spare Toyah !

What do you call a woman having a meal in a restaurant ?

Anita !

What do you call a woman having a meal in a Spanish restaurant ?

Juanita !

What do you call your sister's smelly son ?

My nephew !

What do you call a part-time gas pump attendant ?

Arthur Gallon !

What do you call someone with more money than sense ?

My best friend !

What do you call a fish that tunes pianos ?

A piano tuna !

What do you call a teacher who falls asleep in the class ?

Nothing ! You don't want to wake him up !

Who was the first man to do math ?

Adam !

Who writes joke books in Neverland !

Peter Pun !

NUTTY NAMES

What do you call the brother and sister who like to build things across rivers ?

Archie and Bridget !

What do you call a girl who likes to cook in the backyard ?

Barbie !

What do you call a man with loads of money ?

Rich !

What do you call a man who lies in front of your door all day ?

Matt !

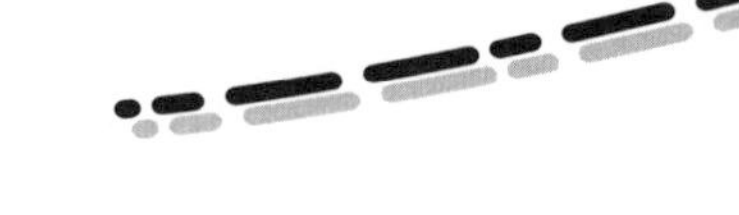

What big cat eats weeds ?

Dan de lion !

What do you call the Gotham City superheroes after they have been run over by a steam roller ?

Flatman and Ribbon !

What do you call a nun with a radio on her head ?

A transister !

What do you call the hairstyle you get from sticking your head in an oven ?

A micro-wave !

What do you call a man who steals cows ?

A beef burglar !

What do you call a dead parrot ?

A polygon !

What do you call joggers in a safari park ?

Fast food !

What do you call a skeleton that refuses to do any work ?

Bone idle !

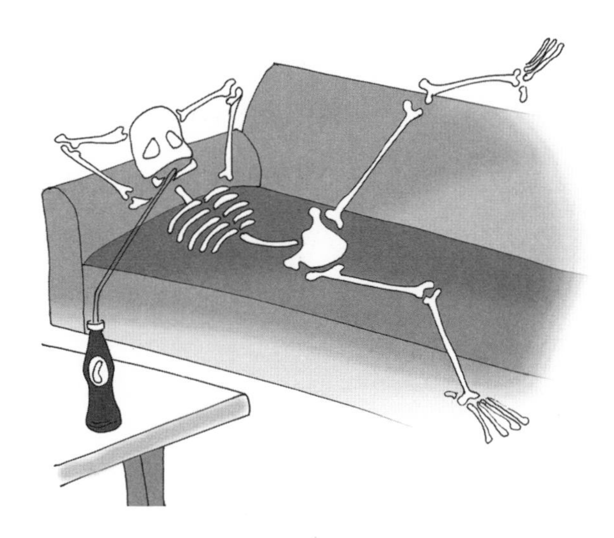

What would you call a band that your dad joined ?

A pop group !

What do you call cattle thieves who wear paper trousers ?

Rustlers !

What do you call a Russian gardener ?

Ivanhoe !

What do you call a woman with a shotgun in her hand ?

Whatever she tells you to, or else !

What do you call the Roman emperor who kept mice ?

Julius Cheeser !

What do you call a woman who was eaten by her cannibal husband ?

Henrietta !

What do you call an ancient Egyptian with no teeth ?

A gummy mummy !

What do you call a frightened man ?

Hugo First !

What do you call a man with an oil rig on his head ?

Derek !

NUTTY NAMES

What do you call a woman who keeps horses ?

Gigi !

What do you call a man with very strong spectacles ?

Seemore !

What do you call a man with a stolen safe on his head ?

Robin Banks !

What do you call a dog that is always rushing about ?

A dash hound !

What do you call a man who delivers Christmas presents to lions and tigers ?

Santa Claws !

What do you call first aid for an injured lemon ?

Lemon aid !

What do you call a man with a duck on his head ?

Donald !

What do you call a vacation resort for bees?

Stingapore !

What do you call a rodent that likes to sword fence ?

A mouseketeer !

What did the Spaniard call his one and only son ?

Juan !

What do you call a girl who comes out very early in the morning ?

Dawn !

What do you call a man with money on his head ?

Bill !

NUTTY NAMES

What do you call a girl with a head made of glass ?

Crystal !

What do you call a lion with toothache ?

Rory !

What do you call a man with a jumbo jet parked on his head ?

Ron Way !

What do you call a dance that snowmen go to?

A snowball !

What do you call a man with an anvil on his head ?

Smith !

What do you call a mad man with the moon on his head ?

Lunar Dick !

What do you call a woman with a boat tied to her ?

Maude !

What do you call a girl with an orange on her head ?

Clementine !

NUTTY NAMES

What do you call a man with a pile of hay on his head ?

Rick !

What do you call a play acted by ghosts ?

A phantomime !

What do you call the ghost that haunts TV chat shows ?

The Phantom of the Oprah !

What do you call a man with a road map on his head ?

Miles !

What do you call a man with a pair of spectacles on his head ?

Luke !

What do you call a vampire with a calculator on his head ?

The Count !

What do you call a man with some cheese on his head ?

Gordon Zola !

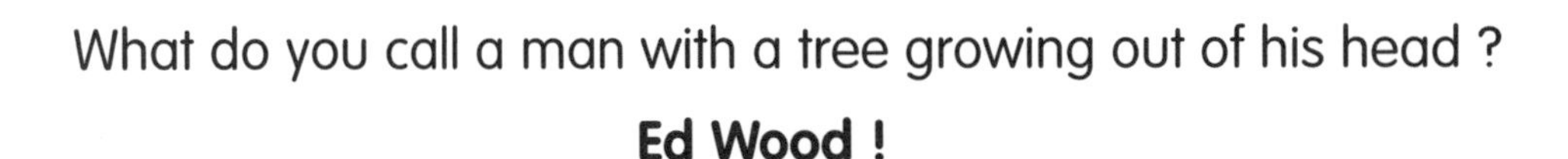

What do you call a man with a tree growing out of his head ?

Ed Wood !

What do you call a nun with a washing machine on her head ?

Sister Matic !

What do you call a witch flying through the skies ?

Broom Hilda !

What did the idiot call his pet zebra ?

Spot !

What was the name of the man who designed King Arthur's round table ?

Sir Cumference !

What do you call a picture painted by an old master ?

An old masterpiece !

What do you call medicine for horses ?

Cough stirrup !

WHO'S ZOO ?

Why do elephants paint their toenails red ?

So they can hide in cherry trees !

What do you get if you cross a cow with a camel ?

Lumpy custard !

Why is the sky so high ?

So birds don't bump their heads !

What's gray and zooms through the jungle at 70 miles an hour ?

An elephant on a motorbike !

How do you stop rabbits digging up your garden ?

Easy—take their spades away !

We call our dog Blacksmith because every now and again
he makes a bolt for the door !

Where do ducks keep their savings ?

In river banks !

Did you know that alligators eat beans for breakfast ?

Human beans, of course !

What lies at the bottom of the sea and shivers ?

A nervous wreck !

Why was Noah able to sail the Ark at night ?

Because it was fitted with floodlights !

Why do bees hum ?

Because they've forgotten the words !

Where do you take an injured wasp ?

To the waspital !

Why do railroad porters like elephants ?

Because they carry their own trunks !

Waiter, bring me an alligator sandwich … and make it snappy !

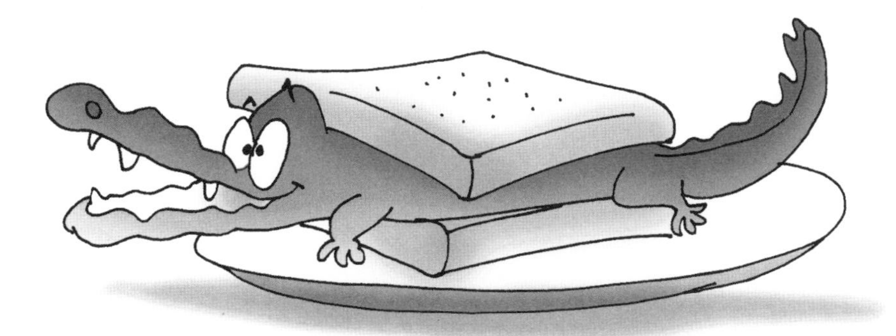

Why did the dinosaur cross the road ?

Because chickens weren't around yet !

Why did the duck cross the road ?

It was the chicken's day off !

Why do elephants have wrinkles ?

Because they hate ironing !

How do you know if an elephant has been in your fridge ?

They leave footprints in the butter !

Why do elephants paint the soles of their feet yellow ?

So they can hide upside down in custard !

What does it mean if you find a set of horse shoes ?

A horse is walking around in his socks !

Why do crabs walk sideways ?

Because they took some medicine which had side effects !

Did you hear about the dog who was too lazy to dig up his bone ?

He was bone idle !

What does a cat rest his head on in bed ?

A caterpillar !

What sort of cat sells wood ?

A catalogue !

What did King Kong say when he was told that his sister had had a baby ?

I'll be a monkey's uncle !

What bulls hide on the riverbank waiting to charge at you ?

Bullrushes !

What's green and highly dangerous ?

A frog with a machine gun !

What's another name for a water otter ?

A kettle !

What's the best way to catch a mouse ?

Get someone to throw one at you !

How do hens dance ?

Chick to chick !

Why do eagles go to church ?

Because they're birds of prey !

What do you call a rich trendy elephant ?

A member of the jumbo jet set !

What do you call a vampire pig ?

Frankenswine !

What do you call sheep that live together ?

Pen pals !

What is the highest form of animal life ?

A giraffe !

What is a vampire's favourite animal ?

The giraffe—it has such a long neck !

What do you call a nervous insect ?

A jitterbug !

What do you get if you cross a giraffe and a dog ?

An animal that chases low flying airplanes instead of cats !

Have you changed the fish's water ?

No, it hasn't drunk the water I put in yesterday yet !

Name four animals from the dog family…

Mommy dog, daddy dog, and two puppies !

Is it true that you can speak cat language ?

Me—How ?

Why did the cow look into the crystal ball ?

To see if there was a message from the udder side !

Why do woodworm have no friends ?

Because they are boring creatures !

What is the most valuable fish ?

The goldfish !

Where do you keep a pet vampire fish ?

In your blood stream !

Doctor, doctor I think I'm an alligator !
Don't worry, Sir. You'll soon snap out of it !

Why are you selling parrots fitted with little alarm clocks ?

Because my wife told me I should go into polly-ticks !

What sort of vacations do animals take ?

They fly by jumbo jet to Moo York !

Why are elephants gray ?

So you can tell them apart from strawberries !

Where do kippers go to be cured ?

To the local sturgeon !

What did the chicken say when the farmer grabbed it by the tail feathers ?

Oh, no! This is the end of me !

How do sheep block the entrance to their fields ?

With a five baaa gate !

Robert, you can't keep a pig in your bedroom—what about the terrible smell ?

Don't worry. He'll soon get used to it !

What is a kangaroo's best sports event ?

The hop-stacle race !

What is gray, has four legs, and a trunk ?

A mouse going on vacation !

What do you get when you cross a skunk with a balloon ?

Something that stinks to high heaven !

What is green and white, and hops ?

An escaping frog sandwich !

Which ballet stars pigs ?

Swine Lake !

Which fish runs the undersea Mafia ?

The Codfather !

Why are herrings such healthy fish ?

Because you never see them ill, only cured !

What do you call a fish that's always asleep ?

Tired !

Roses are red, violets are blue, you look like a trout,
and you smell like one too !

If you use a skunk to catch fish you always
catch them hook, line, and stinker !

Where do dolphins learn ?

In schools, of course !

When fish go on vacation, do they travel on the whale-road ?

What would you eat in a sunken pirate ship takeway ?

Pizzas of eight !

Which sea creatures never go to parties in case they're eaten by mistake ?

Jelly fish !

What do you call a baby turkey ?

A goblet !

Where do fish like going on vacation ?

Finland !

Knock, knock...
Who's there ?
Plaice...
Plaice who ?

Plaice let me in, I'm wet through !

Did you know that fish moms and dads teach their kids not to start eating maggots—in case they get hooked !

Why don't fish play tennis ?

They always get caught up in the net !

What fish can make your feet light up ?

An electric eel !

What do you give a deaf fish ?

A herring aid !

Knock, knock...
Who's there ?

Kipper...
Kipper who ?

**Kipper your mouth shut,
I don't want anyone to know I'm here !**

What sort of fish can you train to fetch your paper every morning ?

A dogfish !

What sort of fish never have any money ?

Poor-poises !

What do you call a lion with no eyes ?

Lon !

Why are fishmongers so unpleasant ?

Because their job makes them sell fish !

What sort of trout can you see after a thunderstorm ?

A rainbow trout !

Why don't sharks eat people in submarines ?

They don't like tinned food !

Who is the most famous cowboy fish ?

Billy the Squid !

What is the best way to get a message to a fish ?

Drop it a line !

Why was the fish sent to jail ?

Because he was gill-ty !

How do fish like their potato chips ?

Ready sea-salted !

Where do fish sleep ?

On a sea bed !

What did the mother whale say to the cry-baby whale ?

Stop blubbering !

What do you have when a rabbit sits on your head ?

A bad hare day !

What weighs two-and-a-half tons, is gray, and floats gracefully through the air ?

A hang-gliding elephant !

What's the worst thing about being a millipede ?

Washing your hands before tea !

WHO'S ZOO ?

What do you call an 85-year-old ant ?

An ant-ique !

What sort of dog has no tail ?

A hot dog !

Why is a cat bigger at night than during the day ?

Because its owner lets it out at night !

What do cats read in the morning ?

The mewspaper !

What did the short-sighted hedgehog say to the cactus ?

Oh ! There you are, mom !

What happens when there's a stampede of cows on the freeway ?

There is udder chaos !

What is gray, has a trunk, and travels at 125 miles an hour ?

A businessman on a fast train !

What is big and gray and has yellow feet ?

An elephant standing in custard !

What is a grasshopper ?

A cricket on a pogo stick !

Which insect can stay underwater for hours at a time ?

A ant in a submarine !

What do you shout to rabbits getting on a ship ?

Bun-voyage !

CRAZY CROSSES

What do you get if you cross a jellyfish with an aircraft ?

A jelly-copter !

What do you get if you cross a kangaroo with a sheep?

A woolly jumper !

What do you get if you cross a vampire with a bowl of soup ?

Scream of tomato !

What do you get if you cross a road without looking ?

Knocked down, stupid !

What do you get if you cross an elephant with a mouse ?

Ten-foot holes in your skirting board !

What do you get if you cross a chicken with a skunk ?

A fowl smell !

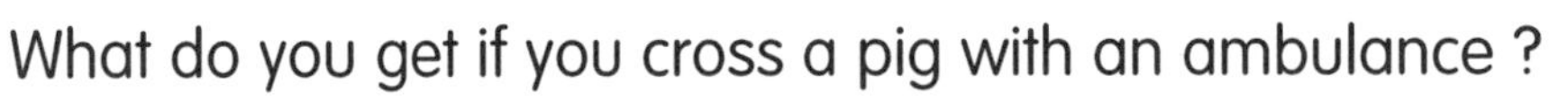

What do you get if you cross a pig with an ambulance ?

A ham-bulance !

What do you get if you cross a pig with Dracula ?

A ham-pire !

What do you get if you cross a chicken with someone who tells jokes ?

A comedi-hen !

What do you get if you cross an explorer with a cat ?

Christopher Columpuss !

What do you get if you cross a cowboy with a dinosaur ?

Tyrannosaurus Tex !

What do you get if you cross the Mafia with a box of teaspoons ?

A gang-stir !

What do you get if you cross a river with a broken bridge ?

Very wet, I should think !

CRAZY CROSSES

What do you get if you cross a sheep with a vacation resort ?

Baaahaaamaaas !

What do you get if you cross a goldfish bowl with a TV ?

Tele-fish-ion !

What do you get if you cross a giraffe and a cow ?

Something you need a ladder to milk !

What do you get if you cross a scary story and a dog ?

Someone who is terrier-fied !

What do you get if you cross a window with a guillotine ?

A pane in the neck !

What do you get if you cross a carrier pigeon and a woodpecker ?

A bird that knocks before delivering the message !

What do you get if you cross a spy and a quilt ?

An under-cover agent !

What do you get when teenage aliens have a party ?

A space racket !

What do you get if you cross a vampire and a boat ?

A blood vessel !

What do you get if you cross a dog with a tree ?

Something with a completely silent bark !

What do you get if you cross a fruit with a tree ?

A pine-apple !

What do you get if you cross a jogger with an apple pie ?

Puff pastry !

What do you get if you cross a kangaroo with a skyscraper ?

A high jumper !

What do you get if you cross an artist with a policeman ?

A brush with the law !

What do you get if you cross a bear with a freezer ?

A teddy brrrrrr !

What do you get if you cross an ice cream with a dog ?

Frost bite !

What do you get if you cross an elephant and a bottle of whiskey ?

Trunk and disorderly !

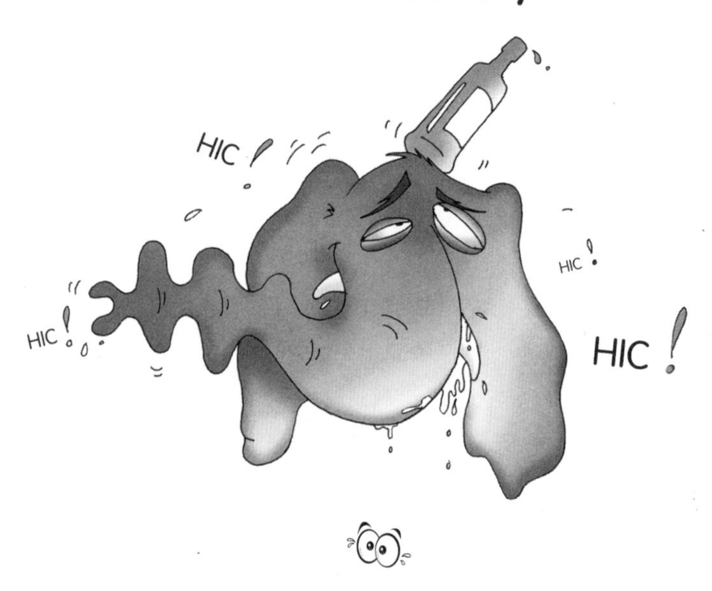

What do you get if you cross a large computer and a hamburger ?

A Big Mac !

What do you get if you cross a TV program and a load of sheep ?

A flock-u-mentary !

What do you get if you cross a toadstool and a full suitcase ?

Not mushroom for your clothes !

What do you get if you cross a dog with a vampire ?

A were-woof !

What do you get if you cross a bike and a rose ?

Bicycle petals !

What do you get if you cross a chicken with a pod ?

Chick peas !

What do you get if you cross an alligator and King Midas ?

A croc of gold !

What do you get if you cross a computer with a potato ?

Micro chips !

What do you get if you cross a cow with a crystal ball ?

A message from the udder side !

What do you get if you cross an alligator with a camera ?

A snap-shot !

What do you get if you cross a vampire with a circus entertainer ?

Something that goes straight for the juggler !

FRIGHT NIGHT

What should you take if a monster invites you for dinner ?

Someone who can't run as fast as you !

Why do vampires write so many letters ?

They have to reply to their fang clubs !

Why are ghosts so bad at telling lies ?

Because you can always see through them !

Mommy, what's a vampire ?

Be quiet dear and drink your blood before it clots !

It's no good locking your door—monsters can always get in.

They have a set of skeleton keys !

What do you call an evil, eight-foot tall, green hairy monster ?

Whatever he tells you to !

What sort of dog would a vampire own ?

A bloodhound !

What did the metal monster have on his gravestone ?

Rust in peace !

Where do vampires keep their savings ?

In a blood bank !

I'd tell you the story of the vampire's broken tooth...

...but there's no point !

A ghost went into a bar at midnight and asked for a whiskey. "Sorry Sir," replied the barman, "we aren't allowed to serve spirits after closing time."

"Doctor," said the cannibal, "I have this terrible stomach ache !"

"Well you must have eaten someone who disagreed with you !"

What is a monster's favorite shape ?

A vicious circle !

Did you hear about the witch who was caught speeding on her broomstick ?

She had a brush with the law !

A vampire's coffin fell off the back of a truck and started rolling down a steep hill. The vampire knew exactly what to do.
He went into a local pharmacy and asked if they had any sore throat sweets to stop his coffin !

What is a vampire's favorite coffee ?

De-coffin-ated !

How do mummies keep a secret ?

They keep it under wraps !

What do you call a ghost's horse ?

A nightmare !

Why do demons and ghouls get on so well together ?

Because demons are a ghoul's best friend !

What tool do ghostly builders use ?

A spirit level !

What do monsters read in the newspaper every morning ?

Their horror-scope !

Who patrols the graveyard at night ?

A fright watchman !

What do you call a ghostly teddy bear ?

Winnie the OOOoooooOooooohHHhhhhh !

What sort of music do mummies like best ?

Wrap music !

Why do skeletons not trust archeologists ?

Because they indulge in skullduggery !

What is a vampire's favorite soup ?

Scream of mushroom !

What sort of pets do monsters keep ?

Ghouled-fish !

What do you call a relaxed ghost ?

Ghoul as a cucumber !

What do Hungarian ghosts eat ?

Ghoulash !

What instrument does a skeleton play ?

A trom-bone !

What is a monster's favorite soup ?

Any flavor, as long as it's a hearty meal !

How can you help a starving monster ?

Give him a hand !

Why didn't the skeleton fight the monster ?

He didn't have the guts !

Why do traveling salesmen always try to sell things to vampires ?

Because they know they're suckers !

What do monsters take to house-warming parties ?

Matches !

Where do you find monster snails ?

On the end of monsters' fingers !

What did the witch say to her cat ?

You look familiar !

What is the essential feature on a witch's computer ?

The spell-checker !

A monster went to his doctor with acid indigestion...
"It's no good," said his doctor, "you'll just have to stop drinking acid !"

A new ghost was sitting in bed reading when an old ghost walked through the wall and into his room.
"It's no good," said the new ghost, "I still don't understand how you do it."
"Watch," said the old ghost, "and I'll go through it again !"

What is the first thing a vampire sinks his fangs into after the dentist has sharpened and polished them ?

The dentist's neck !

What should you do with a green alien ?

Wait until it's ripe !

What do you call an alien with two heads ?

A two-headed alien !

What do aliens do with humans they find in spaceships ?

Put them in the larder—they keep tinned food for emergencies !

Where do aliens live ?

In green houses !

What lights do aliens switch on every Saturday ?

Satellites !

Where do alien children go in the evenings ?

Rocket and roll concerts !

Why are aliens good for the environment ?

Because they're green !

What do aliens call junk food ?

Unidentified Frying Objects !

How do you contact someone who lives on Saturn ?

Give them a ring !

What do aliens have to do before they can drive a rocket at twice the speed of light in deep space ?

Reverse it out of the garage !

What is the quickest way to get an alien baby to sleep ?

Rocket !

What do you call a mad alien ?

A lunar-tic !

Which side of a spaceship passes closest to the planets ?

The outside !

What does an alien gardener do with his hedges ?

Eclipse them every Spring !

Why did the alien buy a pocket computer ?

So he could work out how many pockets he has !

How can you tell if a computer is sulky ?

It will have a chip on its shoulder !

Where do aliens keep fish they capture from other planets ?

In a planetarium !

What do evil aliens grind up to make a hot drink ?

Coffee beings !

Why did the attendant turn spaceships away from the lunar parking lot ?

It was a full moon !

What do you call an alien who travels through space on a ketchup bottle ?

A flying saucer !

How does a martian know he's attractive ?

When bits of metal stick to him !

What do you call a sad spaceship ?

An Unidentified Crying Object !

What do alien children do on Halloween ?

They go from door to door dressed as humans !

How do you know if there is an alien in your house ?

There'll be a spaceship parked in the backyard !

Why are alien gardeners so good ?

Because they have green thumbs !

How do you communicate with aliens out in deep space ?

You have to shout really loudly !

How do you catch a Venusian mega mouse ?

In a Venusian mega mousetrap !

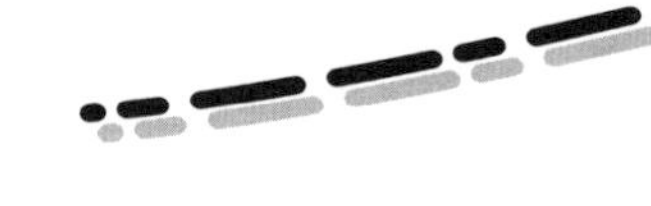

What did the teacher give the alien monster for lunch ?

Class 4B !

How do you invite a robot to a party ?

Send round a tinvitation !

If you get lost in space—who should you ask for directions ?

An alien hairdresser—they know all the short cuts !

If an alien leaves his gum orbiting the Earth—what do you call it ?

A Chew-F-O !

What sort of music do robots like best ?

Steel band music !

Your son will make an excellent rocket pilot !

Why do you say that ?

He has nothing but space between his ears !

Why do steel robots have so many friends ?

I suppose they must have magnetic personalities !

Where is the smelliest part of an alien spaceship ?

The com-poo-ter !

Why did the alien paint his spaceship with sugar and vinegar ?

He wanted a sweet and sour saucer !

How do you tip over an alien spaceship ?

Rocket !

What dance can you see in the night sky ?

The moonwalk !

What is green and very noisy ?

An alien with a drum kit !

Who was the first man on the moon ?

A spaceman !

What is worse than finding a twelve-legged Venusian mega maggot in your apple ?

Finding half a twelve-legged Venusian mega maggot in your apple !

Why do astronauts never eat after take off ?

Because they have just had a big launch !

Why didn't the Martian have his birthday party on the moon ?

Because there was no atmosphere !

How do you know that Saturn is married ?

You can see the ring !

Did you hear about the Martian who went to a plastic surgeon for a face lift ?

She wanted her face to look like a million dollars, so the surgeon made it all green and crinkly !

What do the aliens from the planet Skunkus ride in ?

Phew F-Os !

How did the space aliens go into the space ark ?

R2D2 by R2D2 !

Why did the spaceship land outside your bedroom ?

I must have left the landing light on !

What do you call a space creature that doesn't pass his space exams ?

A fail-ien !

What is the smallest space explorer called ?

A mouse-tronaut !

Knock, knock...

Who's there ?

Jupiter.

Jupiter who ?

Jupiter spaceship on my front lawn ?!

What do you never get if you cross a bug-eyed alien with a dog ?

Robbed !

Why do creatures from the planet THaaarRRgh wear slimy green suspenders ?

To hold their slimy green trousers up !

What goes in one year and out the other ?

A time machine !

If astronauts breathe oxygen during the day, what do they breathe at night ?

Nitrogen !

What do you call a glass robot ?

See-through-P-O !

What does the alien hairdresser do when the shadow of the earth obscures the sun ?

Eclipse !

What do you get if you cross a vampire and a plumber ?

A drain in the neck !

What did the grape say when the space monster trod on him ?

Nothing—he just let out a little whine !

What do you call a noisy spaceship ?

A space racket !

Which part of a space suit is German ?

The helmut !

Which Egyptian king was named after a planet ?

Tutankhamoon !

Why did the alien buy a twisted spaceship ?

He wanted to travel at warp speed !

Why are alien kitchens always such a mess ?

Because of all the flying sauces !

What do you call dishonest spaceships ?

Lying saucers !

What sort of spaceships do secret agents fly in ?

Spying saucers !

What do you call miserable spaceships ?

Sighing saucers !

Why did the alien build a spaceship from feathers ?

He wanted to travel light years !

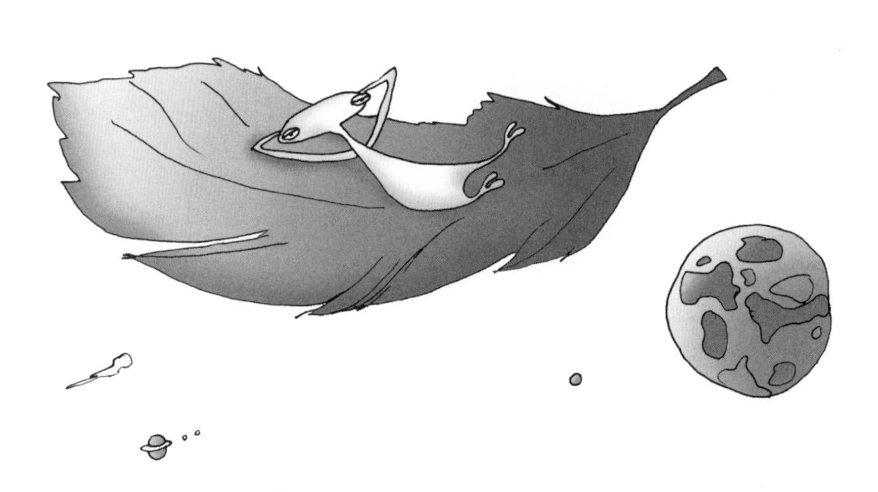

Where do you leave your spaceship while you visit another planet ?

At a parking meteor !

What sort of music do space aliens like best ?

Rocket and roll and heavy metal !

Where do they lock up naughty space creatures ?

Jailien !

What piece of sports equipment does every alien own ?

A tennis rocket !

Why did the alien take a nuclear missile to the party ?

In case he fancied blowing up some balloons !

Why do window cleaners hate vampires ?

They're a pane in the neck !

Why did the vampire go to the blood donor center ?

To get lunch !

Why are owls so brave at night ?

Because they don't give a hoot for ghosts, monsters, or vampires !

What did the old vampire say when he broke his teeth ?

Fangs for the memory !

How do vampires start a duel ?

They stand Drac to Drac !

Why do vampires vacation at the seaside ?

They love to be near the ghostguard stations !

What do you call a futuristic android who goes back in time to plant seeds ?

Germinator !

And what do you call his twin brother ?

Germinator II !

What sort of wolf can you wear ?

A wear wolf !

Why do ghosts catch cold so easily ?

They get chilled to the marrow !

Why are skeletons no good at telling lies ?

Because you can see right through them !

What should you say when a vampire gives you a present ?

Fang you very much !

Why don't vampires like modern things ?

Because they hate anything new fangled !

What do ghosts like with their food ?

A little whine !

Where do vampires like to go on vacation ?

The Dead Sea !

Why did the two vampire bats get married ?

Because they were heels over heads in love !

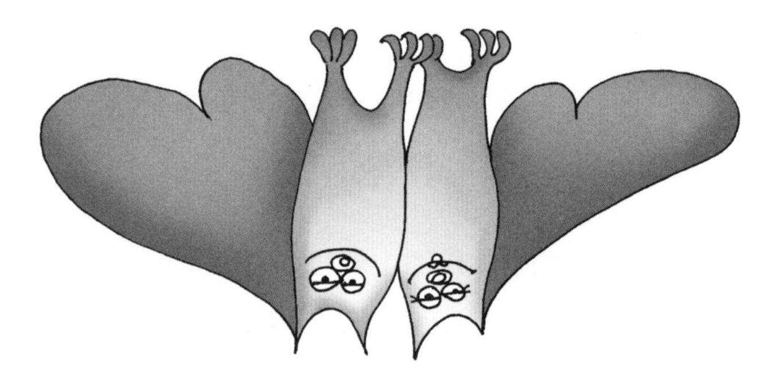

Why did the skeleton fall into a hole ?

It was a grave mistake !

Who delivers Christmas presents to vampires ?

Sack-ula !

Mommy, mommy, what is a werewolf ?

Be quiet and comb your face !

Mommy, mommy, I don't like my Uncle Fred !

Well, just leave him on the side of your plate and eat the fries !

What did the monster say when the vampire asked for his daughter's hand in marriage ?

OK, we'll eat the rest !

Mommy, mommy, I'm just going out for a quick bite to eat !

OK, but make sure you're back in your coffin before daybreak !

What should you wear when you go out for a drink with a vampire ?

A metal collar !

What do you call a young woman who hunts vampires ?

Miss Stake !

What do the police call it when they watch a vampire's house ?

A stake out !

What are the scariest dinosaurs ?

Terror-dactyls !

Why are mummies good at keeping secrets ?

They can keep things under wraps for centuries !

Why is Godzilla sitting on a friend like leaving home ?

Because you end up with a flat mate !

Why do sea monsters go to so many parties ?

They like to have a whale of a time !

During which age did mummies live ?

The Band Age !

Why did the monster comedian like playing to skeletons ?

Because he knew how to tickle their funny bones !

What do monsters have at teatime

Scream cakes !

Which sea monster rules the waves ?

The Cod-father !

What do baby sea monsters play with ?

Doll-fins !

What do monsters call a crowded swimming pool ?

Soup !

How did Frankenstein's monster escape from the police ?

He made a bolt for it !

What sort of music do vampires and ghosts like best ?

Haunted house music !

What sort of jobs do spooks like ?

Dead end jobs !

What do ghosts do at parties ?

They have a wail of a time !

If a monster buys you a chair for your birthday should you accept it ?

Yes—but don't let him plug it in !

Who do vampires invite to their birthday parties ?

Anybody they can dig up !

What is werewolf's favorite film ?

Claws !

KNOCK, KNOCK...

Knock, knock...
Who's there ?
Giraffe...
Giraffe who ?
Giraffe to sit in front of me ?

Knock, knock...
Who's there ?
Superman...
Superman who ?
You know I can't reveal my secret identity !

Knock, knock...
Who's there ?
Adolf...
Adolf who ?
Adolf ball hit me in de mouf !

Knock, knock...
Who's there ?
Police...
Police who ?
Police let me in, I'm freezing out here !

Knock, knock...

Who's there ?

Aliens...

Aliens who ?

Just how many aliens do you know ?

Knock, knock...

Who's there ?

Phil...

Phil who ?

Phil this bag with money, I'm a robber !

KNOCK, KNOCK...

Knock, knock...

Who's there ?

Jim...

Jim who ?

Jim mind if I stay here tonight ?

Knock, knock...

Who's there ?

Frank...

Frank who ?

Frankenstein !

Knock, knock...

Who's there ?

Ivan...

Ivan who ?

Ivan to come in – open the door !

Knock, knock…

Who's there ?

Mike…

Mike who ?

Mike car won't start, can I come in and use the phone?

Knock, knock…

Who's there ?

Avenue…

Avenue who ?

Avenue guessed yet ?

Knock, knock…

Who's there ?

Snow…

Snow who ?

Snow use—I can't remember !

Knock, knock…

Who's there ?

Chester…

Chester who ?

Chester man delivering a parcel !

KNOCK, KNOCK...

Knock, knock...

Who's there ?

Josie...

Josie who ?

Josie any reason to keep me waiting out here !

Knock, knock...

Who's there ?

Boo...

Boo who ?

Don't get upset, it's only a game !

Knock, knock…

Who's there ?

Atilla…

Atilla who ?

Atilla you open this door I'm a gonna stand here !

Knock, knock…

Who's there ?

Alma…

Alma who ?

Alma time seems to be spent on this doorstep !

Knock, knock...

Who's there ?

Wanda...

Wanda who ?

Wanda know how much longer you're going to keep me hanging around out here !

Knock, knock...

Who's there ?

Little old lady...

Little old lady who ?

Your yodelling's getting much better !

Knock, knock...

Who's there ?

McKee...

McKee who ?

McKee doesn't fit !

Knock, knock…

Who's there ?

Mouse…

Mouse who ?

Mouse has burned down—I'm coming to stay with you !

Knock, knock…

Who's there ?

Justin…

Justin who ?

Justin time to let me in !

Knock, knock…

Who's there ?

Josie…

Josie who ?

Josie anyone else out here ?

Knock, knock…

Who's there ?

Paula…

Paula who ?

Paula door open and you'll see !

KNOCK, KNOCK...

Knock, knock...

Who's there ?

Zeke...

Zeke who ?

Zeke and you will find out !

Knock, knock...

Who's there ?

Chas...

Chas who ?

Chas pass the key through the letter box and I'll open the door myself !

Knock, knock...

Who's there ?

Matt...

Matt who ?

Matt as well settle down, looks like I'm in for a long wait !

Knock, knock...

Who's there ?

Zeb...

Zeb who ?

Zeb better be a good reason for keeping me waiting out here !

Knock, knock...

Who's there ?

Polly...

Polly who ?

Polly door handle again, I think it's just stiff !

Knock, knock...

Who's there ?

Greta...

Greta who ?

Greta friend like that again, and you'll end up with none at all !

Knock, knock...

Who's there ?

Paul...

Paul who ?

Paul the door open for goodness sake !

Knock, knock...

Who's there ?

Woody...

Woody who ?

Woody open the door if we asked him nicely ?

Knock, knock...

Who's there ?

Kline...

Kline who ?

Kline of you to invite me round !

Knock, knock...

Who's there ?

India...

India who ?

India is some of my stuff, and I've come to collect it !

Knock, knock...

Who's there ?

Alvin...

Alvin who ?

Alvin your heart—just you vait and see !

Knock, knock...

Who's there ?

Candy...

Candy who ?

Candy owner of this big car come and move it off my drive !

Knock, knock...

Who's there ?

Chuck...

Chuck who ?

Chuck the key under the door and I'll let myself in !

Knock, knock...

Who's there ?

Khan...

Khan who ?

Khan you give me a lift to school ?

Knock, knock...

Who's there ?

Colin...

Colin who ?

Colin in for a chat !

Knock, knock...

Who's there ?

Wendy...

Wendy who ?

Wendy you want me to call round again ?

Knock, knock…

Who's there ?

I know kung fu…

I know kung fu who ?

I'd better not upset you then !

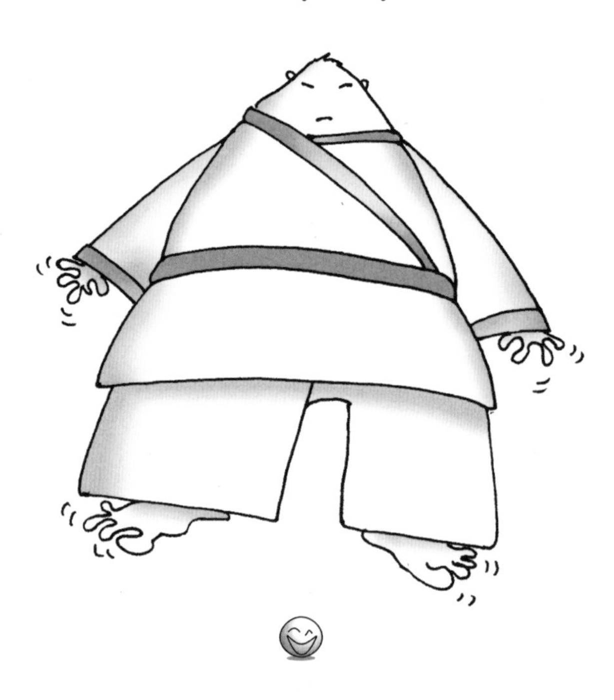

Knock, knock…

Who's there ?

Cohen…

Cohen who ?

Cohen to knock just once more, then I'm going away !

KNOCK, KNOCK...

Knock, knock...

Who's there ?

Kent...

Kent who ?

Kent you stop asking questions and open the door !

Knock, knock...

Who's there ?

Ahmed...

Ahmed who ?

Ahmed a big mistake coming here !

Knock, knock...

Who's there ?

Ginger...

Ginger who ?

Ginger hear the doorbell ?

Knock, knock...

Who's there ?

Courtney...

Courtney who ?

Courtney door, can you open it and let me loose ?

Knock, knock...

Who's there ?

Isabelle...

Isabelle who ?

Isabelle not working ?

Knock, knock...

Who's there ?

Guess Simon...

Guess Simon who ?

Guess Simon the wrong doorstep !

Knock, knock...

Who's there ?

Amos...

Amos who ?

Amos-quito is chasing me—please let me in !

DETENTION SPAN

Bill, how do you make a Mexican chilli?

Take him to the South Pole, Miss!

Teacher: Joe, give me a sentence with the word detention in it !

Joe: I had to leave the horror film before it had finished, because I couldn't stand detention !

For tonight's homework I want you to write an essay on a goldfish.

I can't do that, Sir !

Why on earth not ?

I don't have any waterproof ink !

Sally: Sir, my parents want me to tell you that they were really pleased with my last report.
Teacher: But I said you were a complete idiot !
Sally: But it's the first time anyone in our family has been really good at something !

Principal: What do think about in the school vacation ?
Pupil: I never think about schoolwork !
Principal: Not really much of a change for you then ?

Teacher: Name a bird that doesn't build its own nest.
Sally: The cuckoo.
Teacher: That's right! How did you know that ?
Sally: Everyone knows that cuckoos live in clocks !

DETENTION SPAN

Teacher: Ben, if five cats were on a bus and one got off,
how many would be left ?

Ben: None, Sir !

Teacher: How do you get that answer ?

Ben: Because the other four were copycats !

Teacher: Who can tell me which sea creature eats its prey two at a time ?

Student: Noah's Shark !

What's the difference between a bird watcher and a teenager ?

One gets a hide and spots, the other gets a spot and hides !

Why were ancient sailing ships more ecofriendly ?

Because they could go for hundreds of miles to the galleon !

Teacher: Joe, I do wish you would pay a little attention !

Joe: I'm paying as little as I can, Sir !

Teacher: Did you find the exam questions easy ?

Bill: Oh, yes I found the questions all right. It's the answers I couldn't find !

Teacher: Mary, why was no one able to play cards on Noah's Ark ?

Mary: Because Noah stood on the deck !

Teacher: John, name me a famous religious warrior !

John: Attila the Nun ?

DETENTION SPAN

Teacher: Did you know that most accidents happen in the kitchen ?

Student: Yes, but we still have to eat them !

Teacher: Who was Thor ?

Student: The god who kept thcratching hith thpot !

Teacher: How do you cure lockjaw ?

Student: Swallow a key ?

Teacher: If you had to multiply 1,345 by 678 what would you get ?

Student: The wrong answer !

NEW BOOKS IN THE GEOGRAPHY LIBRARY…

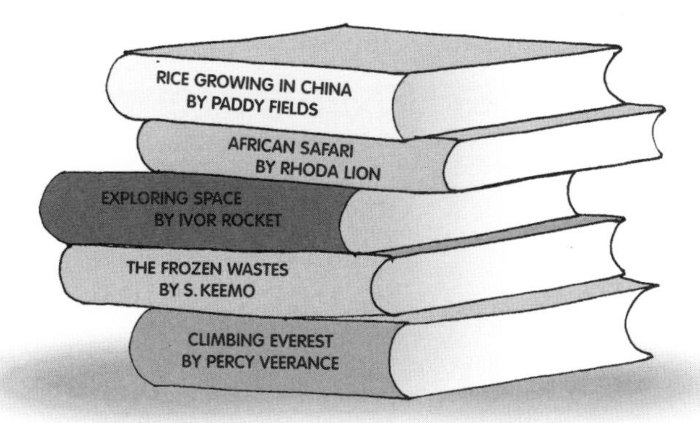

John: Dad, have we got a ladder ?

Dad: What do you need it for ?

John: For homework. I have to write an essay on an elephant !

Teacher: Jim, what is the largest species of mouse in the world ?

Jim: The hippopota-mouse !

Teacher: Sarah, what evidence is there that smoking is harmful to the health ?

Sarah: Well, just look what happened to all the dragons !

ANIMAL SCHOOL REPORTS...

Cheetah: A nice enough boy, but not to be trusted.

Leopard: Has missed a lot of classes this year due to spots.

Hyena: Seems to think that everything is a joke.

Stick Insect: Never been the same since the elephant mistook him for a pencil !

Teacher: Why were you late for school today, Carol ?

Carol: I got a flat tire on my bicycle !

Teacher: Did you run over some broken glass ?

Carol: No, Sir, there was a fork in the road !

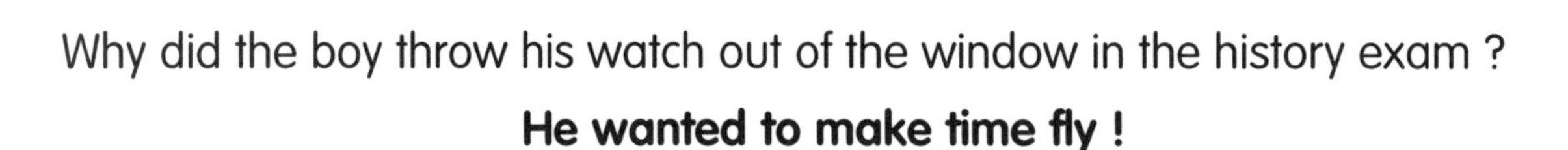

Why did the boy throw his watch out of the window in the history exam ?

He wanted to make time fly !

Teacher: Steven, what's a computer byte ?

Steven: I didn't even know they had teeth !

You have a photographic memory, Jane.

It's a shame that nothing ever develops !

Teacher: Joe, give me a sentence with the word counterfeit in it.

Joe: I wasn't sure if she was a centipede or a millipede so I had to count her feet !

Computer teacher: Sally, give me an example of software.

Smith: A floppy hat ?

Teacher: How would you stop a cockerel waking you at 5 a.m. ?

Student: Eat him for supper before you go to bed !

Teacher: Ben, give me a sentence with the word illegal in it !

Ben: My Dad took me to the bird hospital the other day and we saw a sick sparrow and an illegal!

Teacher: Who discovered Pluto ?

Student: Walt Disney ?

Joe, why are you looking in lost property ?

My grandma moved house last week and I can't remember where she lives now !

Teacher: Today we're going to look for the lowest common denominator…

Student: Haven't they found that yet ? My Dad says they were looking for that when he was at school !

Parent: Do you think my son will make a good Arctic explorer ?

Teacher: I would think so, most of his marks are below zero !

Teacher: Please don't talk while you are doing your exam !

Student: It's all right, Miss, we're not doing the exam—just talking !

Why are math teachers no good at gardening ?

Because everything they plant grows square roots !

Did you hear about the math teacher whose mistakes started to multiply ?

They took him away in the end !

Sally, how do you make a milk shake ?

Take it to a scary film, Miss !

Joe, do you understand how important punctuation is ?

Yes, Miss, I always make sure I get to school on time !

Jane, when do you like school the best ?

During the school vacation, Sir !

Bill, how did Moses cut the sea in half ?

With a sea-saw ?

Joe, which part of a fish weighs the most ?

The scales, Sir ?

Name me someone who has been around the globe ?

Terminator, Miss !

Who on earth is Terminator ?

My goldfish !

John, shouldn't you wash your hands before you start your piano lesson ?

No, Miss, I only play on the black notes !

Now, can anyone tell me what Egyptian kings were buried with ?

Yes, Miss, they were buried with their Nammaforrs !

What is a Nammaforr ?

Knocking nails in !

Ben, how can you prove that the earth is round ?

I didn't say it was, Sir !

What did you think of your first day at school Joe ?

First ?! You mean I have to go back again !

AARDVARK TO ZOOM

A

Aardvark	A vark that thinks it's tough
Abigail	Strong wind heard in a monastery
Absent minded	Oh ! I seem to have forgotten this one
Absolute	The best musical instrument in the world, ever
Accidental	When you fall and knock your teeth out on the way to the dentist's
Aromatic	Early machine for making arrows
Attendance	Dance for 10 people
Audio visual	Sign language
Automate	When your best friend is a robot

B

Backgammon	Game played by pigs
Baked Alaska	The result of global warming
Bandage	The average age of a pop group
Banshee	Don't let that ghost in here
Barber	Sheep trained as a hairdresser
Barbecue	An outdoor party for sheep
Beehive	What mommy bees tell naughty bees to do
Bird of prey	Eagle that goes to church every Sunday
Blockade	Stop lemonade being delivered
Blood brother	Vampire's relative

C

Campus	Cat that lives in a college
Caterpillar	Where a cat sleeps
Chatterbox	A box that can't keep a secret
Cheapskate	Skateboard for a budgerigar
Chilli powder	Fine snowflakes
Christmas Island	Where Santa spends the Summer ?
Cliff hanger	Where a giant leaves his coat
Cloak	A Chinese frog's mating call
Coat of arms	Monster's coat with 13 sleeves
Comb	Something you part with but never give away
Crime wave	Where robbers go to surf

D

Dandruff	Mrs. Druff's husband
Dark Ages	A time when there were lots of nights
Deadline	Fence around a graveyard
Defence	Something that runs round the backyard
Depend	The end of the swimming pool with most water
Dessert spoon	Spoon for eating sand
Disconcerted	Thrown out of a concert
Dogmatic	Robot dog

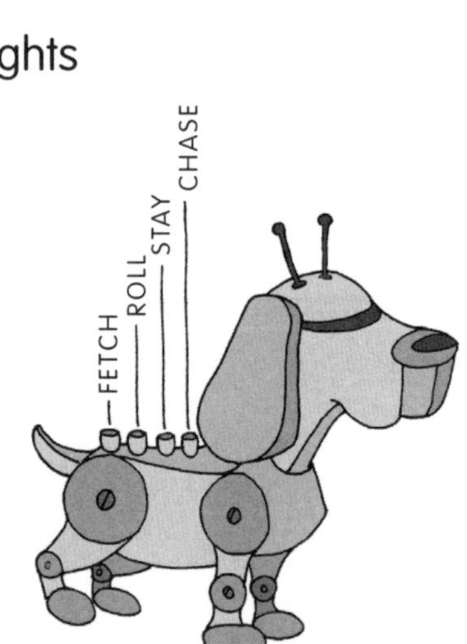

E

Earwigs	Hair that old people grow out of their ears
Eclipse	A haircut booked on the Internet
Effortless	Sleeping through an exam
Elderberry	Oldest berry on the plant
Electric eel	Fish that swims in strong currents
Emulate	Ostrich pretending to be an emu
Engraving	Vampire's hobby
Experiment	What scientists did 100 years ago and you are still doing in school
Explosion	Result of experiment
Eyecatching	Game played by monsters

F

Fail safe	Safe with a broken lock
Falsehood	A fake hat
Family tree	Place where ghouls bury each other for a laugh
Father-in-law	Dad in jail
Feedback	When a vampire bites you from behind
Fertile	Tiles in a werewolf's house
Fetlock	Padlock for a horse
Fireworks	Sack everybody in the factory
Flashback	What happens when you hold the camera back to front
Flight deck	The pack of cards used by pilots
Fly by night	Vampire owl
Flying colors	Paint thrown in art lesson
Foul-mouthed	Bad language from a chicken

G

Galleon Fuel measure for old ships

Gamekeeper Teacher who confiscates computer games in class

Generation gap The distance you keep behind your parents when they do something embarrassing

Gherkin Relatives of a gher

Gladiator How a monster felt after lunch

H

Hair restorer Veterinarian

Harvest What farmers wear to cut corn

Heart warming Monster's cooking class

Heirloom Weaving machine for rabbits

Homesick Bored with being at home over the Summer

Honeycomb What bees use to style their hair

Humbug Insect that can't remember the words

Hysterical Funny version of history

Icicle A bicycle with a bit missing

Ideogram Telegram sent to an idiot

Identical Twins who laugh at the same time when you tickle them

Illegal A sick bird of prey

Illiteracy Disease caught from books

Ignite Eskimo's bedtime

Impatient Someone fidgeting in the doctor's waiting room

Impeccable Hidden away from birds

Impediment Broken bicycle

Incas The first people to write with fountain pens

Introduce Orange drink served at start of match

Ivanhoe A Russian gardener

Jargon A missing jar of strawberry jam

Jitterbug Tense insect

Joan of Arc Noah's mom

Joint account The bank where Frankenstein keeps all his spare parts

Juggernaut Empty jug

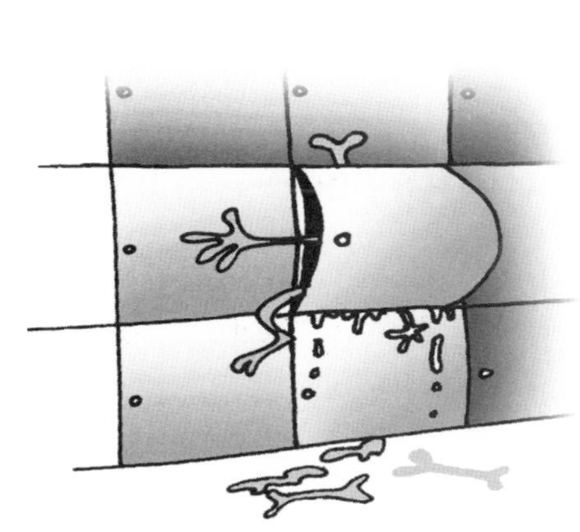

Karate	Self-defense for rats
Kenya	Can you ?
Kettle drum	What musicians make tea in
Kidnap	Sleeping baby
Kipper	Fish that is always asleep

Korma	What you end up in if someone drops a pan of curry on your head

L

Labrador	Large cat-flap for dogs
Lambda	Greek letter invented by a young sheep
Lapdog	Greyhound used in racing
Last minute	Longest 60 seconds of the whole school day
Launch pad	Throw notebook at someone
Lazy bones	Idle skeleton
Lie detector	Principal

M

Macintosh	Waterproof computer
Magic eye	What teachers have in the back of their heads
Mental cruelty	Double math on Friday afternoon
Mermaid	A deep-she fish
Milk chocolate	Something that no one can do
Milk shake	What you get from nervous cows
Misprint	Copy someone else's homework incorrectly
Mitten	What a cat has when it swallows a ball of wool
Moment of truth	Exam results
Moonbeams	They hold up the moon
Mummy	Egyptian child's daddy
Mumbo jumbo	Elephant who doesn't speak clearly

N

Nag	Tell off a horse
Narrow minded	What you are when you have a splitting headache
Near miss	Avoid bullies by standing close to the teacher
Neck line	Vampire's target
Neptune	Song heard under water
Nerve cell	Where naughty nerves are kept in prison
Nickname	Someone called Nicholas
Nightmare	Vampire horse
Numbskull	Very cold skeleton

O

Octopus	Cat born in October
Odin	Noisy god
Offenbach	Noisy dog
Offish	When you only want to eat meat
Olive oil	Stops olives going rusty
Optical	Tickle an opera singer
Organ grinder	Monster with food processor
Out of bounds	Escaped from prison
Outside broadcast	Shout through window
Overcast	Throw fishing rod into middle of river

P

Palatable	Tasty table for monsters to eat
Paperweight	Heavy school bag
Parapet	Pet parrot kept by parachutist
Parity	Two parrots exactly the same
Password	Hand a note to someone in class
Perspex	Plastic spectacles
Phoney	Fake mobile phone
Physiotherapy	Medicine mixed with lemonade

Picador	Choose an entrance to a bullfight
Pigment	Paints for pigs
Pigswill	How a dead pig leaves things to his family
Ping-pong	Table tennis played by skunks
Pizzicato	Pizza for cats
Plasma	Mom made by a plastic surgeon
Pole vault	Where the expensive poles are locked away
Polygon	Missing parrot
Punch line	End of a boxing joke

Quadruped	Bicycle with four pedals
Quicksand	Sand that runs away when you're not looking
Quicksilver	Money that's easy to spend
Quiz master	Ask teacher questions he can't answer

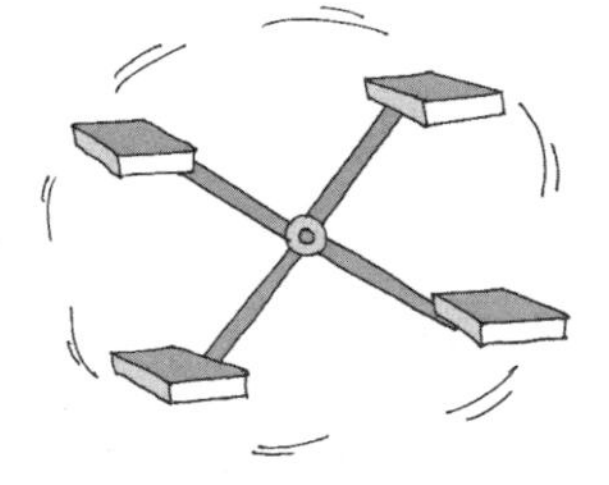

Rainbow	Bow tie for a raindrop
Remorse	Send coded signal again
Road hog	Pig driving badly
Rush hour	When bullrushes go home from work
Rustler	Woman in a paper dress

S

Sandbank — Where camels keep their savings

Sandpaper — Newspaper designed to be read on the beach

Scrapbook — List of fights you've been in

Seasickness — What a doctor does all day

Sharp-witted — Someone with a pointed head

Skullcap — What a skull boy wears

Slippers — Shoes made from banana skins

Snowball — Formal event for snowmen and women

Sourpuss — Cat that eats lemons

Split pea — Pea with a split personality

Spongecake — What jellyfish eat at parties

Staple diet — Eating small bits of bent metal

Steel wool — What you get from robot sheep

Stereotype — Type using two fingers

T

Tangent — Man who has been out in the sun

Test pilot — Someone who makes paper airplanes out of his test paper

Three-legged race — What monsters win on their own

Time machine — Spaceship full of herbs

Towel — Gets wetter the more it dries

Transparent — Glass Mom or Dad

Tuning Fork — To make sure your musical chairs are all in tune

Undercover Spy hidden under your quilt

Unlucky Running into a vampire when you're trying to escape from a werewolf

Unplug What you should do with an electric chair before you sit down

Viper A wash cloth

Vulgar fraction A fraction with bad manners

Watchdog A dog that can tell the time

Water bed Where crabs sleep

Water polo What horses play in the swimming pool

Water table Where fish eat their meals

Wear and tear What oversized monsters do with their clothes

Weight watcher Someone who looks at his stomach in the mirror all day long

Witchcraft Broomstick

Wolf whistle What a fox referee uses

Wonkey Unsteady donkey

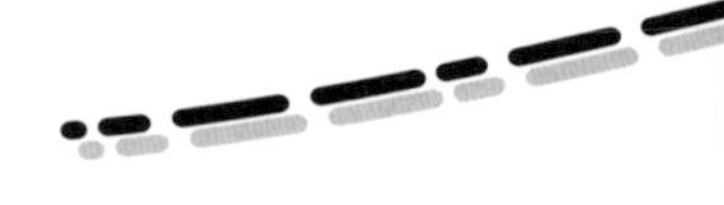

XYZ

Xylophone What you use to telephone someone on the planet Xylo

X-ray The ghost of Ray

Yellow fever Illness you get from eating too many bananas

Yolks Jokes told by chickens

Zermatt What you wipe zer feet on
Zinc Where you wash your hands
Zing What you do with zongs in a choir
Zoom lens The sound of a camera falling from a great height

BRAINTEASERS

How do you stop a head cold going to your chest ?

Easy—tie a knot in your neck !

Why shouldn't you try to swim on a full stomach ?

Because it's easier to swim on a full swimming pool !

What creature sticks to the bottom of sheep ships ?

Baaa-nacles !

How do you know if your little brother is turning into a fridge ?

See if a little light comes on whenever he opens his mouth !

What is the coldest part of the North Pole ?

An explorer's nose !

Why is honey scarce in Brazil ?

Because there's only one B in Brazil !

How did the witch know she was getting better ?

Because the doctor let her get out of bed for a spell !

What did the witch call her baby daughter ?

Wanda !

How do witch children listen to stories ?

Spellbound !

What would you find in a rabbit's bank account ?

Bucks !

Why can you never swindle a snake ?

Because it's impossible to pull its leg !

Why is it easy to swindle a sheep ?

Because it is so easy to pull the wool over its eyes !

What did the overweight ballet dancer perform ?

The dance of the sugar plump fairy !

What do elves eat at parties ?

Fairy cakes !

Why did the carpenter go to the doctor ?

He had a saw hand !

What do you call a deer with no eyes ?

No idea !

What is the only true cure for dandruff ?

Baldness !

What should you buy if your hair falls out ?

A good vacuum cleaner !

What sort of fish would you find in a bird cage ?

A perch !

What sort of fish would you find in a shoe ?

An eel !

How do you swim 100 yards in two minutes ?

Over a waterfall !

Did you hear about the dog who was arrested ?

He didn't pay a barking ticket !

Did you hear about the bungee jumper who shot up and down for three hours before they could bring him under control ?

He had a yo-yo in his pocket ?

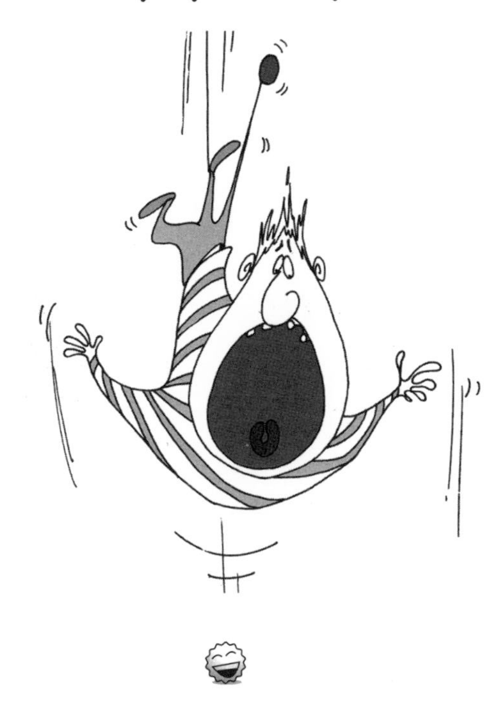

What book do you buy to teach children how to fight ?

A scrapbook !

What sort of animals make the best TV presenters ?

Gnus-readers !

How is your other invention coming along—you know, the matches ?

Oh ! They've been a striking success !

I once met a man from Hong Kong,
Who'd been jogging for twenty years long.
He was terribly sweaty,
He looked like a yeti,
And his feet had a terrible pong !

I hear you've just invented gunpowder ?

Yes, I was using some candles to light my laboratory and it came to me in a flash !

Why did the doctor take his nose to pieces ?

He wanted to see what made it run !

Why do pens get sent to prison ?

To do long sentences !

What was the parrot doing in prison ?

It was a jail-bird !

What sort of animal is best at getting up in the morning ?

A llama clock !

What is the name of the detective who sings quietly
to himself while solving crimes ?

Sherlock Hums !

Why did the farmer feed his pigs sugar and vinegar ?

He wanted sweet and sour pork !

Which French city has the best stock of paper?

Rheims !

Why is the soil in my backyard always dry ?

Because you have leeks !

What did the little boy say when he wanted his big brother to give him back his building bricks ?

Lego !

What gets smaller the more you put in it ?

A hole in the ground !

Waiter, why is there a dead fly in my soup ?

Well, you surely don't expect to get a live one at these prices !

What happened to the man who stole a truck load of eggs ?

He gave himself up—he said he only did it for a yolk !

Stop ! This is a one-way street !

Well, I'm only going one way !

Yes, but everyone else is going the other way !

Well, you're a policeman, make them turn around !

How do penguins get to school ?

On 21-speed mountain icicles !

Why do cows have horns ?

Because they'd look pretty silly with bells on their heads !

What goes MOOOOOZ ?

A jet flying backwards !

Why do toolmakers always escape from fires ?

They know the drill !

What did the bull say when he came back from the china shop ?

I've had a smashing time !

What self-defense method do mice use ?

Ka-rat-e !

What did the stupid burglar do when he saw a "WANTED"
poster outside the police station ?

He went in and applied for the job !

BRAINTEASERS

What is a big game hunter ?

Someone who can't find the baseball stadium !

What is the difference between a cookie and an elephant ?

You can't dip an elephant in your milk !

Why were the naughty eggs sent out of the class ?

For playing practical yolks !

Why did the bakers work late ?

Because they kneaded the dough !

How many monsters would it take to fill this room ?

No idea, I'd be gone after the first one arrived !

How does Santa Claus start a joke ?

This one will sleigh you... !

What jewelry do ghosts wear ?

Tombstones !

How can you sleep like a log ?

Put your bed in the fireplace !

What can you catch and hold but never touch ?

Your breath !

Who is the biggest gangster in the sea ?

Al Caprawn !

What do you do if a ghoul rolls his eyes at you ?

Just pick them up and roll them back !

BRAINTEASERS

Why did the man jump up and down after taking his medicine ?

Because he forgot to shake the bottle before he took it !

Which famous artist had a bad cold ?

Vincent van Cough !

Why did the burglar buy a surf board ?

He wanted to start a crime wave !

Why don't pigs telephone one another ?

Because there is too much crackling on the line !

Why are pigs no good at do-it-yourself ?

Because they're ham-fisted !

Why did the burglar break into the music shop ?

He was after the lute !

What does a toad use for making furniture ?

A toad's tool !

What does a toad sit on ?

A toadstool !

Why did the burglar break into the bakers ?

He wanted to steal the dough !

How do you keep a fool in suspense ?

I'll tell you tomorrow !

How do you make a fool laugh on Saturday ?

Tell him a joke on Wednesday !

Where would you find a bee ?

Near the start of the alphabet !

What do you call a letter when it's dropped down the chimney ?

Blackmail !

Why did the burglar go to the bank ?

To recycle his bottles !

What does it mean if your nose starts to run ?

It's trying to catch a cold !

Why is the leopard the only animal that can't hide from hunters ?

Because it's always spotted !

Who is a caveman's favorite band ?

The Stones !

Why did the elephant refuse to play cards with his two friends ?

Because one of them was lion and the other was a cheetah !

Why does a giraffe have such a long neck ?

Have you ever smelled a giraffe's feet !

What jungle animal would you find at the North Pole ?

A lost one !

What sort of frog is covered in dots and dashes ?

A morse toad !

BRAINTEASERS

Where do cows go for history lessons ?

To a mooseum !

What does a polar bear use to keep his head warm ?

A polar ice cap !

What do you get if you cross a group of stars with a silver cup ?

A constellation prize !

What do owls sing when it's raining ?

Too-wet-to-woo !

What do you need to electrocute an orchestra ?

A good conductor !

How do teddies like to ride horses ?

Bear back !

What do teddies take when they are going on vacation ?

Just the bear essentials !

Waiter, there's a small worm in my salad !

Oh dear, I'll tell the chef to send you a large one !

Who always puts thyme in his soup ?

A clock mender !

Why are those clothes running out of the sports shop ?

They're jogging suits !

BRAINTEASERS

What sort of fruit would you find in a diary ?

Dates !

Why do cows lie down together when it rains ?

To keep each udder dry !

What sort of ghosts haunt hospitals ?

Surgical spirits !

When should you put your electric guitar in the fridge ?

When you want to play some really cool music !

Which is the greenest city in Europe ?

Brussels !

Which Italian city is good for wandering round ?

Rome !

Why are bearded men fearless ?

Because they can never have a close shave !

What do you get if you cross a skunk with an owl ?

Something that stinks, but doesn't give a hoot !

Why do vampires like crossword puzzles ?

They like the cryptic clues !

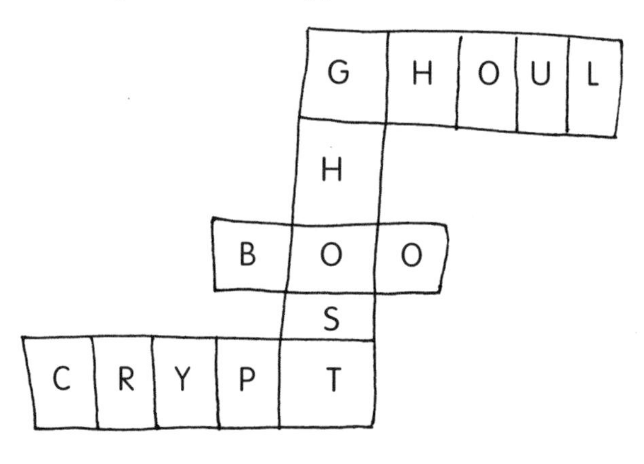

Where do vampires go on vacation ?

Vein-ice !

Who did the vampire marry ?

The girl necks door !

What do cannibals do at a wedding ?

They toast the bride and groom !

Why is the bookshop the tallest building in the town ?

Because it has the most stories !

Why must you always have holes in your socks ?

You wouldn't be able to get your feet in them if you didn't !

In which battle was Alexander the Great killed ?

His last one !

In which film does fruit rule the world ?

Planet of the grapes !

Which of these is correct:

"Egg yolk is white"

"Egg yolk are white"

Neither—egg yolk is yellow !

What goes up but never comes down ?

Your age !

What music does King Neptune like ?

Sole !

Why does it snow in the winter ?

Because it's too hot in the summer !

Why is it impossible to open a locked piano lid ?

Because all the keys are on the inside !

How do you measure the size of fruit ?

With a green gauge !